HORSES

Above: This handsome Canadian working horse in full harness and padded collar
has such neat ears and refined head that it probably has Oriental origins.
Overleaf: A herd of horses cooling off in the midsummer heat.

HORSES

Angela Sayer

Contents

Left: Harness racing at St. Moritz, Switzerland, on a track covered with hard-packed frozen snow and sheet ice. This sport demands a highly skilled driver and an agile, sure-footed horse.

This book was devised and produced by
Multimedia Publications (UK) Ltd

Editor **Richard Rosenfeld**
Design **Behram Kapadia**
Picture Research **Jessica Johnson**
Production **Arnon Orbach**

ISBN 0-8317-4556-8

First published in the United States of America 1984 by Gallery Books, an imprint of W. H. Smith Publishers Inc., 112 Madison Avenue, New York, NY 10016

Originated by D S Colour International Ltd, London
Typeset by Rowland Phototypesetting (London) Ltd
Printed in Spain by Cayfosa, Barcelona
Dep. Legal B-30.102 - 1984

Introduction

Cave paintings, drawings on pottery, sculptures and tapestries from many countries, as well as countless references to the horse in literature, show how the various breeds of today developed through the centuries.

Herds of wild horses were to be found throughout Asia and Europe in prehistoric times. One ancient breed, which was isolated in the remote Great Gobi desert for hundreds of years, has remained almost unchanged to the present day; it is still skittish, watchful and shy of man. Known as the Przewalski, after the explorer who discovered the breed, it can be found in small herds in captivity in such places as Marwell Park in Britain and the Wildlife Park north of San Diego, California.

Today's descendants

Most of today's heavy breeds are descended from the Przewalski, while the finer-boned Arabians and Thorough-breds are descended from the Tarpan. The Tarpan breed evolved when the Great Ice Age forced the northern forest horses southward, where they interbred with horses of the plains.

Horses were domesticated sometime between 3000 and 2000 BC. The people of the Nile tamed the African Wild Ass to carry packs, and the Sumerians trained the Asiatic Wild Ass to draw war chariots. The Mongolians were the first people to mount and ride the tough, wiry horses of the plains and deserts. They used them to herd their cattle and for attacking other tribes.

Beauty, skill and speed

From these beginnings the horse has been bred for various qualities of color, size, shape and ability. Today, of course, technology has largely taken over the business of transport-ation, although there is no vehicle that can beat the horse when it comes to crossing rough terrain. Much of the animal's popularity lies in its contribution to sporting events – racing, dressage and jumping. The combination of beauty, skill and speed that the animal displays in performance is a guaranteed crowd-puller. But above all, perhaps, the horse's worth lies in the unique relationship that develops between it and its rider, as anyone who has been riding – whether pony trekking or steeplechasing – will testify.

Left: Australian Kevin Bacon comes to grief on Chichester, as he fails to clear a particularly formidable obstacle in the Olympic arena in Montreal, Canada, during the 1976 Games.

Foals

Foals are young horses – the male is a colt foal, the female a filly foal. If the colt is not to be used for breeding purposes later in life, it is castrated at an early age, becoming a more manageable and easily trained gelding. The filly is mature at four years of age, when she becomes a mare. Although mares are generally more temperamental, many people prefer owning, training and riding them. Also, once the female's working days are over, she is able to reproduce.

Birth of a foal

Before breeding, the mare must be pronounced healthy and fit by a veterinarian. The stallion too, must be chosen with great care. After mating the foal is carried for 11 months. Most births are fairly easy. Usually the mare will seek out clean pasture in a sheltered field. Within a few moments of birth, the foal struggles to its feet and attempts its first, wobbling steps. The young animal is nuzzled and cleaned by its mother, who encourages it to feed on her rich milk, and although at first the foal's legs seem too long and ungainly to stand, it has them under control within a few hours. Soon, the foals will gambol and play, rather like young lambs, learning to run, turn sharply, buck and kick. Grazing nearby, the mares keep a watch on their offspring and gallop to their defence at the first sign of danger.

Growing up

The foal continues to feed on its mother's protein-rich milk long after it is grazing efficiently. In a wild herd she will often be accompanied by her yearling from the previous breeding season, as well as the current year's foal. The wild stallions fight for supremacy and the privilege of serving the mares in each group, and usually drive off colts reaching maturity. These break away to form bachelor herds. In this way, only the fittest bloodlines are conserved.

The foal of a "domestic" horse is usually weaned at about six months of age, being raised with other foals until it is nearly two years old. Depending upon its type or breed, it will undergo various degrees of training. The thoroughbred will be sufficiently developed to start racing at this early age, although a horse intended for riding will not be worked under saddle until it is four.

Left: One of the hardiest Pony breeds is the tiny Shetland, which grows to an average height of 40 inches. Shetlands developed in the islands of the same name, off northern Scotland.

Left: When a foal is born in a protected environment, the mare gets to her feet very soon after the birth then licks and cleans the foal's coat. This loving attention from the mare encourages the foal to struggle to its feet in a very short time.

Below: A foal born in the wild immediately forms a close relationship with its mother and the rest of the herd.

Above: A foal is one of the most appealing of all baby animals. Despite the slenderness of its limbs, it will soon be strong enough to gallop beside its mother whenever she bolts from possible danger.

Left: The mare's bag is situated between her hind legs. The mare relaxes the hind leg opposite the side on which the foal approaches her, so that it can suck easily. While her foal feeds, the mare keeps a constant watch for signs of approaching hazards or possible danger.

Below: A magnificent Shire mare grazes peacefully alongside her leggy young foal. Shires, like most heavy horse breeds, make good mothers and produce great quantities of milk in order to build the characteristic massive bones. A gelding will eventually weigh about 1 ton, being capable of hauling extremely heavy loads.

Above: A caring, superb Welsh Cob mare is moving her foal away from harm. The Welsh Cob is the largest of the four Welsh Pony breeds and makes a fine general purpose or family riding pony, suitable for hacking, hunting or club events. It is unrivaled as a riding or driving pony.

Right: Safe and relaxed in the close presence of its mother, a New Forest Pony foal dozes in the sunshine. Though these ponies live in semi-wild herds in the great tracts of scrub and forest land of southern England, they actually belong to local people. Bays and browns predominate but the ponies can be almost any color.

Above: A Palomino mare with glowing, guinea-gold coat and flaxen mane and tail grazes alongside her filly foal. The foal's juvenile coat is pale cream, but already the true golden tone is showing through on her legs and muzzle. Palominos only show their true coloring in the summer. The winter coat is pale cream.

Left: A Dartmoor mare and foal. Originally used as a mining pony, drawing heavy loads of coal. It is a particularly attractive breed with a beautiful head and small, alert ears. Gentle-natured, quiet and patient, it is ideal for children.

14

Above: Another Palomino foal, this one is sheltering in an Australian eucalyptus grove. Its coat is molting – it should be the color of a newly minted gold coin, with pure white mane and tail.

Left: The foal is able to graze soon after birth, but it has to splay its long limbs well apart in order to reach the ground. Although it grazes constantly throughout the day, the foal will continue to feed from the mare at regular intervals until it has been weaned.

Above right: Whenever possible, mares and foals should be turned out together in a large paddock. Mares enjoy the company and their foals gain a great deal from play sessions with other young horses. These two young Hungarian foals spar playfully as they test one another's reflexes and reactions, rearing and pretending to bite at muzzle, nose and neck.

Right: Adult horses of the Camargue district in the South of France are light gray. Like the offspring of many gray breeds, however, the foals are often a much darker color at birth, the gray coat developing gradually. This foal's true color is beginning to show through at the end of his muzzle.

Around the World

Today, there are over 200 breeds of horses throughout the world, and all are descended from four basic types – the Forest horse, which was usually found in fairly cold, wet climates and was a sturdy animal with large head and feet; the Steppe horse, a small light horse with long legs which inhabited the warmer climates of northern Africa and Asia; the Plateau horse, which roamed over Europe and northern Asia; and the Tundra horse of the Polar regions.

Despite extensive crossbreeding which has taken place over the centuries, descendants of these ancient breeds still exist, including the Mongolian Przewalski and the Tarpan.

Wild horses too, still abound. Some of the most exciting are the sturdy Brumbies of Australia, the gray Camargue horses of France, the Mustangs of North America the Icelandic ponies, and the ponies of the British Isles. Many of these are descended from domesticated animals which escaped captivity and returned to their natural habitat.

Cold Bloods and Hot Bloods

Horses are generally referred to in two groups, the Cold Bloods and Hot Bloods. These names have nothing to do with blood temperature but with temperament. The Cold Bloods include the heavy horses, used mainly for draughts purposes, while the Hot Bloods include the fiery Arabians and Thoroughbreds. The intermediate Warm Bloods are produced by crossing the two and have moderate temperament. They are neither as lively as the Thoroughbreds nor as sluggish as the draught horses.

Versatile and indispensable

The horse is a creature of great versatility – whether pulling a plough or brewery dray; performing in circuses and rodeos, or assisting the police and military.

The most highly trained horses in the world come from the Spanish Riding School in Vienna. Originally, the institute was for teaching cavalry officers to ride. The rigorous training schedule lasts three years and at the end of it the animals are capable of precise and elegant movements and stunning feats calling for outstanding courage from horse and rider alike.

Left: The spirited Kathi mounts of these Indian lancers were obviously picked for their good looks, agility and obedience. The Arab influence is evident in the slightly inward pointing ears.

Left: Wild horses vie for dominance over a man-made waterhole in Montana. Horses naturally form small, close herds, each with one stallion, a harem of mares, foals and yearlings. Such herds normally keep to their own ranges, but when food or water is in short supply, the stallions may fight for watering rights.

Below: Two rodeo riders compete in the steer wrestling contest. The rider on the left of the picture keeps the steer running in a straight line, enabling his partner to draw alongside, leap onto and wrestle the steer to the ground. Each pair is timed and the fastest pair wins.

Right: Argentinian gauchos are probably the most skilled riders in the world. Their favorite mount is the Criollo, descended from the Argentine Mustang – strong, stocky and able to withstand extremes of climate. Here, gauchos move a herd of Brahman cattle to new grazing grounds.

Below: Horses were introduced to the Americas by the Spanish conquistadores in 1511 when Hernan Cortez landed with his men and their mounts. Some horses turned wild (feral), and eventually there were herds of them, known as Mustangs. The North American Indians captured and tamed them and, in due course, some were used for cow herding. Here, cowboys round up a herd.

Above: Mostly descended from Barb ("Barbary") horses, the Spanish Andalucian and Austrian Lippizaner are renowned as classical riding horses.

They are slow to mature and train easily. Here, Patricia Findlay schools her great gray Andalucian horse from the Iberian Peninsula.

Above: The Lippizaner is the best known of all Austrian breeds because of its performances in the Spanish Riding School of Vienna. It was originally bred in a district near Trieste, highly valued by the ancient Greeks as excellent horse-breeding territory. This agile stallion is being trained to perform a series of sophisticated high school, or *haute école*, movements.

Right: Three great stallions on display at the Pompadour State Stud Farm in France. The Postier Breton is a square-set, strong and active horse, similar in type to the English Suffolk Punch. The French Ardennais dates back to Roman times and probably formed the foundation stock for the Great Horse or English Black of the Middle Ages.

Left: Sure-footed Haflinger ponies draw a sledge through the snowy Austrian countryside. These ponies are always chestnut-colored and generally have a light mane and tail. Haflingers are short-legged and so strong that they are used for a variety of agricultural tasks and on mountainous routes, as well as for riding.

Below: A French horseman with his fine young Pottok stallion. In the background, a stud farm tucked away in the hills in Pays Basque. The French countryside has always been ideal for breeding and raising horses. The lush pastures, rich in minerals and salts promote the development of strong bones.

Right: A peaceful pony grazes, surrounded by cattle egrets on the Island of Chincoteague, off the coast of Virginia. On Pony Penning Days, the last Thursday and Friday each July, the semi-wild Chincoteague ponies are rounded up to swim the channel across to the neighboring island of Assateague, where the annual pony sale is held.

Below: The tough and wiry native South American ponies are renowned for their stamina and sure-footedness over difficult terrain. Although they are small, they are capable of carrying an adult and packs many miles each day. They are also ideal for herding cattle. This dun pony works high in the Chilean uplands.

Above: A trio of Indian mounted police displaying their Kathi mounts' agility as they charge at full gallop, lances at the ready.

Right: A blindfolded and well-padded old horse waits patiently in the bull-fighting arena. His splendidly attired rider will goad and excite the bull when it first enters the ring. The picadors and matadors (out of the picture) watch the bull's reactions to see which horn he uses most and in which direction he attacks.

Below: A young Hungarian showing a novel way of schooling a pair of horses. Hungary has an excellent tradition as a horse breeding nation. One of its most famous breeds is the Shagya Arabian.

Left: Viennese carriages, or *fiacres*, carry tourists who prefer a foot-resting way of viewing the city's multitude of treasures. The carriages are traditionally drawn by well-matched ponies in smart, highly-polished harness. The wear and tear of the hard streets on the horses' legs is barely concealed by bandaging.

Left: A string of Kirghiz horses toil to the top of a barely marked trail through a mountain pass in the Soviet Union. A native of the U.S.S.R., the Kirghiz has remarkable strength and stamina for its size. It is so sure-footed that it is ideal for pack work and carrying substantial loads through mountainous regions.

Right: A magnificent pair of dappled gray Shire horses, complete with decorated harness, await their turn to parade with a brewery dray (wagon) at the annual Harness Horse Parade, in London's Regent's Park. The great Shire is apparently descended from the Great Horse of Chivalry, used by medieval knights. These horses are still used for heavy farm work.

On Parade

One of the most exciting aspects of any military or ceremonial parade is undoubtedly the horse. The well-groomed beast is nearly always the focal point, particularly when its rider is in brightly-colored, full uniform. The sheer size and stateliness of this one image makes it an unrivaled, breathtaking spectacle.

Training

A great deal of effort goes into preparing horses for parading. The calmness of these beautiful animals in the face of cheering, flag-waving crowds and flash-bulb photography is achieved through a gruelling training schedule which lasts for one year. During this time the horse is exposed to the type of situation it will encounter while on parade: brass bands, milling crowds and so on. Gradually, over the months, the animal becomes accustomed to noise and clamor and learns to remain passive and to respond only to the commands of its rider.

Of course, not every horse is suitable for parading; a highly-strung animal, for example, would not be chosen. Above all, steadiness is the quality that is looked for when selection is being made. The horse, which will usually begin its training when three years old, must also be good-natured, obedient and, not least, comfortable to ride.

The animals must look magnificent too, and an enormous effort goes into grooming before the parade begins. Their flanks are brushed, their manes and tails combed and their shoes checked, oiled and polished.

It is not only the horses that have to be schooled – the riders also undergo a training programme. After all, it can't be easy sitting still in a saddle with back straight and eyes forward for hours on end!

The Spanish Riding School

The most highly trained horses in the world come from the Spanish Riding School in Vienna. Originally, the institute was for teaching cavalry officers to ride. The rigorous training schedule lasts three years, and at the end of it the animals are capable of precise and elegant movements and stunning feats that call for courage from horse and rider alike. One of the most impressive and balletic manoeuvres that is taught involves the horse leaping high in the air with forelegs tucked in and hindlegs outstretched, while the rider remains upright with back straight. It is the pinnacle of a horse's ceremonial training.

Left: A stunning turnout of cavalry as the Queen's Troop carry out their drill in London's Hyde Park.

Above: After the July 1981 wedding of Prince Charles and Princess Diana in London, the couple returned to Buckingham Palace in an open carriage drawn by these magnificent Windsor Greys.

Right: Even perfectly trained parade horses can bolt. During the pageantry of the Royal Wedding, one of the Life Guard troop's mounts broke into an excited gallop, almost unseating his rider. The amused crowds, waiting for the Royal entourage, reach for their cameras.

Below: Along the Wedding route, waiting crowds first see two phalanxes of great gray London police horses, followed by a troop of Life Guards in full ceremonial dress and mounted on matching blacks. Finally, the carriage bearing the bride and groom, with the handsome Windsor Grays up front.

Left: Trooping the Color, on the official birthday of the British monarch. Here, the mounted brass band is lead by a magnificent drum horse. It has been trained to move sedately and is guided by reins attached to the stirrups, leaving his rider's hand free to beat the drum.

Below: An impressive troop of the Royal Canadian Mounted Police parade at the annual Calgary Stampede. The "Mounties" are now so highly mechanized that their carefully selected and trained horses are used mainly to perform the troop's famous Musical Ride.

Right: A Lippizaner stallion performing in the great hall of the Spanish Riding School in Vienna, inaugurated by Emperor Charles V in 1570. He imported the best horses from all over the world to form his own breeding stud. The Lippizaner is descended from the Spanish Andalucian horse, which gave the school its name.

Below: A troop of lancers parades before the Presidential Palace in New Delhi. The well-matched mounts are probably descended from the Australian Waler valued for its strength and courage. Many thousands of Walers were shipped to India during the First World War for military use. Australian quarantine rules prevented their repatriation.

Above: A well-matched team of brilliantly plumed, Akhal-Teke Liberty horses perform at the Moscow State Circus. Though inclined to obstinacy, this breed's action is showy and ideal for a circus.

Right: A delightful Palomino pony in full parade gear. Palomino horses are popular as parade or circus animals because the golden coat, offset by the flowing white mane and tail, can be groomed to perfection.

Below: Members of the Royal Canadian Mounted Police display team taking part in their famous Musical Ride. Here, lances in the presented position, they pass in pairs between the lines of their comrades, in the movement called the Bridal Arch. Other sections of the Ride are known as the Maze, the Dome and the Shanghai Cross.

Left and right: Jousting today is a popular entertainment, similar in most respects to jousting in medieval times. The only missing ingredient is that the "knights" don't kill each other any more as frequently happened.

Left: Today, there are several societies that train members and their mounts in the arts of medieval fighting. Great attention is paid to correct dress and accoutrements for the horses, as well as to weaponry and jousting techniques. Modern jousting tournaments are a popular draw at agricultural shows and county fairs, providing an enormous amount of excitement.

Left: This Japanese archer is mounted on a small, speedy Hokaido pony, a tough and fearless animal descended from the Mongolian Wild Horse. It is very similar to the Chinese pony, arguably faster than the Arabian over a short distance. Hokaido ponies were extensively used by the mounted police of Tokyo until 1874.

Below: The traditional sport of Yabusame, dating back to the Samurai warriors of the eleventh century, is still a popular attraction at Japanese outdoor events. Dressed in traditional costumes, and riding well-schooled horses, the Yabusame archers must use unwieldy, ancient bows to shoot their arrows at specific targets, while riding at full gallop.

Right: A rider dressed in fifteenth century Samurai costume, and carrying a traditional bow, rides his gray to the starting line to take part in the Yabusame contest.

Winning

Flat racing is often called the "Sport of Kings" because it was due to royal patronage in England during the seventeenth century that the Thoroughbred – the universal racehorse of today – evolved.

In America, racing was begun by early settlers who matched their work horses against one another, but today it has become a popular sport. The top flat race in America is considered to be the Belmont Stakes, run at Belmont Park, and two other classic races for top Thoroughbreds are the Kentucky Derby and the Preakness Stakes.

Hurdle racing

Racing over jumps became fashionable long after flat racing was established, but today's Grand National Steeplechase, held in England, near Liverpool is the most famous race in the world. In the U.S., the great steeplechase is the Maryland Hunt Cup. It is actually hurdle racing, seen less in Britain and in Europe.

Harness racing, in which horses trot or pace around tracks while their jockeys sit in very light, two-wheeled carts called sulkies, is particularly popular in France and the U.S., and also practiced in Sweden and Britain. Specially bred horses are used for trotting, and some countries have developed their own distinctive breeds.

English classics

England has several world-famous racecourses, including the great track at Newmarket in Suffolk, the home of the English Thoroughbred. Ascot in Berkshire was founded by Queen Anne in 1711. The Derby, held annually at Epsom, is run over 1½ miles and forms the cornerstone of the English classic season which starts with the 2000 Guineas race over one mile at Newmarket early in the year, and finishes with the St. Leger run over 1¾ miles at Doncaster, Yorkshire in September.

Only one horse has been talented enough to win all three races in recent years, and this was the great Nijinsky who won the Triple Crown in 1970.

In Europe, France is the main home of racing and produces superb horses. The Longchamp course on the outskirts of Paris was opened in 1857 and is the venue of the traditional annual Grand Prix de Paris.

Left: Horse racing, as this photograph shows, is incredibly demanding for both rider and mount.

Steeplechasing was originally a rural competition, run across fields, over fences and ditches from one village church to the next. Steeplechasing today is much more demanding, as this sequence shows, sometimes involving multiple pile-ups.

Right: As horse number 16 makes a bad mistake and unseats his jockey, the following horse in blinkers tries to swerve in midair. Unfortunately, his momentum carries him into the leading horse, and his jockey tumbles down to join the first as yet another horse jumps blindly into the mêlée *(center)*. Finally, a third horse unseats its rider who is about to join the other two on the ground as they roll, to protect themselves from the flying hooves *(far right)*.

Right: As they pass the winning post, jockeys put everything they have into producing the best possible finish from their mounts, extracting the last ounce of effort right up to the line.

Above: In hurdle racing the horses take the obstacles at high speed. Such racing demands horses with courage, stamina and an excellent turn of speed. Here, four horses fight it out at Kempton Park, England, although generally in Britain steeplechasing is a much more popular sport.

Left: The moment that makes it all worth while! A proud owner leads in her winning horse, American Beldale Ball, the American winner of the 1980 Melbourne Cup.

Above: Approaching the finishing line at the famous British race course at Goodwood known as "glorious Goodwood," the two leaders drive their mounts for first place.

Above: Snowy divots fly as these Thoroughbreds race around a bend in the track and head for the winning post during a race meeting at St. Moritz, the Swiss sporting center.

Right: Teams of horses race over a snow-covered Swiss track. They have been unharnessed from their lightweight racing carts and, instead, drag along their drivers on skis.

Below: Goggled to protect their eyes against the glare and glancing ice crystals, five jockeys race their mounts abreast, into the closing stages of a fast and furious hard-fought race at St.Moritz, Switzerland. Racing on snow and ice is extremely exciting for participants and spectators alike. The horses' hooves need special protection to prevent them from sliding.

Above: Harness racing has become popular in many countries, some of which have developed breeds for trotting and pacing. The American Standardbreds either trot or pace, the two gaits being inherited then encouraged by training. The Standardbred was named after the breed's requirement to race over a measured distance within a standard time before it could be officially registered.

Right: Tiny Falkland ponies gallop at high speed around the track, with their drivers in lightweight, Ben Hur-style chariots behind. Harnessed four abreast, the ponies are specially trained to pull together.

Below: Among the many and varied events staged at Canada's exciting Calgary Stampede is the chuck wagon race, in which matched teams of four strong horses negotiate the wide course at speed. Each team is accompanied by three outriders, who encourage their own side and no doubt hinder the opposition. Like all rodeo events, this is potentially dangerous.

Going for Gold

Show jumping is one of the most popular and spectacular of all equestrian sports. A comparatively recent sport, it combines speed, daring, precision and all the color, glamour and suspense that accompanies such a highly competitive and potentially lucrative event.

Great demands are made on horse and rider in the light of such pressures. It is essential that the horse possesses an equable temperament – if it is nervous it is unlikely to be able to cope with the tension of a major competition. The horse's head is a good indication of its personality and temperament. The eyes should be bold and large, and the ears active and alert, showing interest and intelligence.

Dressage and eventing

Though it lacks the excitement of show jumping and eventing, dressage boasts a grace and style of its own, which hypnotizes and delights its audience. The key factors are natural balance and controled movement. Dressage was developed from the fine horsemanship displayed by the medieval knights, with horse and rider carrying out a series of exact movements which show the horse's lightness, suppleness and obedience. The horse moves smoothly forwards, backwards and sideways, turning, changing direction, stopping and starting. Dressage is seen at its most advanced in the Spanish Riding School of Vienna.

Eventing competitions are perhaps the most formidable tests of horse and rider, and are derived from the training and exercises carried out by cavalry officers. Today, they are one- or three-day affairs, involving grueling cross-country rides over considerable distances and testing obstacles, a dressage test and a show jumping course. Both horse and rider are tested fully to their limits for fitness, speed and endurance.

Olympics

Whether the competition is show jumping, dressage, or eventing, the greatest ambition of most riders is to take part in the Olympic Games. Winning is obviously important but the Games also give riders from all over the world the chance to meet and test their own skills and that of their mounts at world class standards.

Left: The American Michael Matz and his fine bay gelding Jet Run exemplifying the concentration needed to win a major show jumping event.

Left: One of show jumping's most celebrated obstacles is the Derby Bank, constructed at the permanent show ground at Hickstead in the south of England. A test of ability in even the greatest of show jumpers, the bank must be executed with perfect timing, precision and control. As few owners can build anything approaching this obstacle, horses may face it at Hickstead without adequate practice.

Below: Indoor jumping competitions call for a horse to jump accurately and precisely, and to make tight controled turns without losing impetus. This horse is clearing the jump efficiently and in good style and, with ears pricked, is already looking forward to the next obstacle in line.

Above: British rider Jane Stroud proves that it is not always as easy as it looks when her horse Fanta misjudges the parallels at Hickstead and drops his hind legs between the poles.

Above: This perfectly groomed horse, Warwick Rex, ridden by Alwin Schockemöhle, takes off over a 1976 Montreal Olympic fence, watched by hundreds of spectators in the arena and by millions on television.

Right: Great skill is required to prepare a horse for a major event. Fitness must be achieved slowly and methodically so the animal reaches its peak at the right time for the competition. The rider, too, must be in top condition, and both must have complete accord, with an almost telepathic understanding of each other's requirements and aims.

Below: The Olympic Games in Munich, 1972, provided a superb show jumping course, expertly planned and meticulously laid out in order to exact the best performance from each contestant. The spectators were obviously enthralled by the style and ability of this beautiful bay horse as he confidently cleared the parallel poles.

Above: A high-performance horse clearing a big jump
with grace, ability and obvious enjoyment. His rider
has good style and balance in spite of the fact that he is
losing his left stirrup iron.

Above and Right: The famous obstacle known as the Trout Hatchery at the Burghley Horse Trials, England, attracts huge crowds of spectators as they can be certain that a fair proportion of competitors will land in the water.

The shallow, reed-fringed lake is spanned by a tree trunk on one side, over which the horse is required to jump cleanly into the water. After passing through the lake the horse must then jump a low but solid obstacle back onto dry land and the remainder of the course. Horses are often reluctant to jump into water, and refuse, coming to an abrupt halt like Castlewallan, seen here tipping his rider into the lake.

Left and Below: Two different approaches to the same jump in the Crosscountry phase of a Three-day Event. Eventing is testing for both horse and rider, pushing them to the limits of their stamina and ability. The first day consists of dressage, followed by the demanding cross country phase on day two and a precise show jumping component on the third day.

Top right: Gatcombe Park, the country home of Princess Anne and Captain Mark Phillips is regularly used to stage horse trials. Well-designed obstacles are constructed and facilities provided for the crowds of visitors who come to see top riders negotiating the demanding course.

Right: Lucinda Prior-Palmer on the great chestnut eventer Be Fair demonstrates just how it should be done. Be Fair's first major victory was in England at Badminton in 1973 after which event he was selected for the European Championship team in Kiev. He carried Lucinda to her first European title in West Germany in 1975, but retired after injury in 1976.

Above: Polo was brought to England via India in 1869, and to the U.S. in 1880. It remains a popular equestrian sport. Conducted at high speed, each play period or chukka lasts only about eight minutes with each match consisting of four, six or eight chukkas. Specially bred polo ponies are used.

Left: In driving championship competitions, presentation and appearance is as important as performance, and this four-in-hand turnout is certainly very impressive. The driver, known as the "whip", is required to show his team's paces in the ring at the trot, changing direction as requested by the judges, before they assess general presentation of team and vehicle.

Left: An entrant in the combined driving event negotiates a particularly testing hazard during the crosscountry phase, trying desperately to keep the vehicle from veering off a straight line behind his tandem-hitched ponies. The final phase of such an event consists of negotiating a series of tight turns and narrow openings marked by bollards within the show ring.

Picture Credits

All-Sport Trevor Jones 46 top   **Animal Graphics/Solitaire** 8-9, 10 top, 14, 16, 29   **Animal Photography** 24 top   **Ardea** 13 top, 18-19, 22, 23 bottom, 24 bottom, 25 top, 26, 51 top   **Bruce Coleman** 13 bottom, 15, 17 bottom, 21 bottom, back endpaper   **Gerry Cranham** 6-7, 27 top, 44-45, 46 bottom, 47, 55, 56, 57, 61 bottom   **Daily Telegraph Colour Library** 32   **Robert Estall** 1, 37 bottom   **Robert Harding Picture Library** 11   **David Higgs** 60   **Alan Hutchison** 21 top, 25 bottom, 28 top, 28 bottom   **Impact Photos** 33   **Oxford Scientific Films** 10 bottom, 20 top   **Rex Features** 61 top   **Mike Roberts** 2-3, 4-5, 30-31, 44 top, 45 top right and left, 49 top, 59, 63   **Tony Stone Photolibrary-London** 12 bottom, 37 top, 38, 39, 52-53, 54 top, 64   **Vision International** 36, 40, 41, 49 bottom, 50, 62   **ZEFA** front cover, back cover, front endpaper, 12 top, 17 top, 20 bottom, 34, 35, 42-43, 48, 51 bottom, 54 bottom, 58

Multimedia Publications (UK) Limited have endeavored to observe the legal requirements with regard to the rights of the suppliers of graphic and photographic materials.

Back jacket: Horse and rider in perfect unison at Hickstead, England 1980.

Back endpaper: A delightful collection of Hungarian thoroughbreds.